R AMAZING! ™

We find the amazing in the ordinary everyday with lists, polls and quizzes. Helping us to appreciate, in fun and quirky ways, the world in which we live.

Creating interactive content, R Amazing! is a safe place to explore different topics and share your views.

It is ok to disagree with us regarding who or what we think is amazing! We share our thoughts on our website and in our books to enable debate and discussion.

We encourage the expression of opinions in an appropriate way with an understanding that it is ok for people to have differing views.

R Amazing! debates should be conducted politely and respectfully, ending with an agreement and common ground, even if that is to agree to disagree.

www.r-amazing.com

Sharks R Amazing!
Mark 'Markus' Baker & Adam Galvin

Published by R-and-Q.com.
Copyright © 2020 R-and-Q.com

SHARKS

R AMAZING! ™

www.r-amazing.com/sharks/

Adam Galvin and Markus Baker
Creators of R Amazing!

"*Sharks aren't the monsters we make them out to be*"

Yasmine Hamdi

"

Books are sharks because sharks have been around for a very long time. There were sharks before there were...

...dinosaurs, and the reason sharks are still in the ocean is that nothing is better at being a shark than a shark.

Douglas Adams

"

More Deadly Than sharks

We tend to imagine that sharks are one of the most deadly animals to humans because we hear a lot about them attacking. This, however, is not true.

Surprisingly, other animals are far more dangerous than sharks who kill around six people each year worldwide. Whereas cows cause twenty-two deaths per year. Deers, on the other hand, as a result of causing car crashes, take the lives of around one hundred and thirty people annually. However, it is hippos who are the most deadly of all, with around two thousand nine hundred yearly fatalities in Africa alone.

> *Many people continue to think of sharks as man-eating beasts. Sharks are enormously powerful and wild creatures, but you're more likely to be killed by your kitchen toaster than a shark!*
> Ted Danson

Extra Senses

Along with vision, taste, hearing, touch and a great sense of smell, sharks have two additional senses called electroreception and lateral lines.

Using tiny receptors that sit in jelly-filled sensory organs called the ampullae of lorenzini and positioned close to their nostrils, sharks can pick up small electrical signals around them. Electroreception makes it easier for sharks to find their prey.

Sensing vibrations in the water using their lateral line system, sharks can receive changes in the strength and angle of the water vibrations around them. This enables them to find injured prey that are creating waves from their distress. It likely sharks attack us because they mistakenly believe human swimmers or surfers are struggling in the water. After that first bite they realise there error, because research shows sharks dislike the taste of humans.

The only thing on the mind of a shark is to eat.
Dwayne Carter Jr

DID YOU KNOW?

Shark expert Daniel Bucher's research shows that humans taste horrible to sharks. Which is why they let us go when they realise that we are not the prey they expected. This may also explain why people tend to have a single shark bite rather than many bites.

There are around 5 – 10 shark related deaths each year, over 100 million sharks are murdered each year. Now, who's the killer?

Unknown

LEARN MORE AT

www.r-amazing.com/hammerhead/

Hammerheads

With its unique shaped head, it is easy to see why they are called Hammerhead sharks. A head that is perfectly designed to pick up electrical fields in the ocean with its 3,000 ampullar pores. This helps them to find stingrays who are usually hiding beneath the sand.

Research from 2009 discovered that a Hammerhead shark can see 360 degrees because their eyes are placed on the tips of their head. This placement also enables an amazing binocular vision to see at long distances.

*The eyes of Hammerhead sharks
are tilted slightly forward, allowing
the field of vision of each to
significantly overlap.*
BBC Earth

How Old?

Working out the age of a shark is said to be similar to the way that you can tell how old a tree is, by counting the number of rings on the tree's stump.

On a shark, you use their backbones, called vertebrae. Each bone has see-through bands that pair together. So if, the vertebrae have 6 bands, it is fair to guess that the shark is around 6 years old.

However, recent research suggests that this way of working out the age of the shark is not always correct and there needs to be a more accurate and precise way of calculating their age.

Don't let anyone tell you you're too young to do something. A baby shark is still a damn shark.
Unknown

What's scarier than an ocean with sharks? An ocean without them.
Greenpeace

DID YOU KNOW?

Tonic immobility is when a shark goes into a trance-like state. This is done by flipping a shark upside down or through stimulation to the sensor pores on their snout. Both methods help scientists subdue sharks when handling them for research. A word of caution, this hypnotic sleep works on most sharks and rays, but not all of them.

Shark Tagging

Through connecting a tracking tag to the dorsal fin of a shark and then releasing it back into their natural habitat, researchers can start to learn more about these amazing and secretive animals. Scientists can see where the shark is, its movement and migration patterns.

There is even an app called Expedition White Shark that lets you track Great White sharks live to your phone or tablet. Where along with the researchers you can discover that Great White sharks in the Eastern Pacific Ocean often swim between Mexico and Hawaii, which is nearly 1000 miles in distance.

Sharks are the balance keepers of the ocean and the path to healthy, abundant oceans goes through them.
OCEARCH

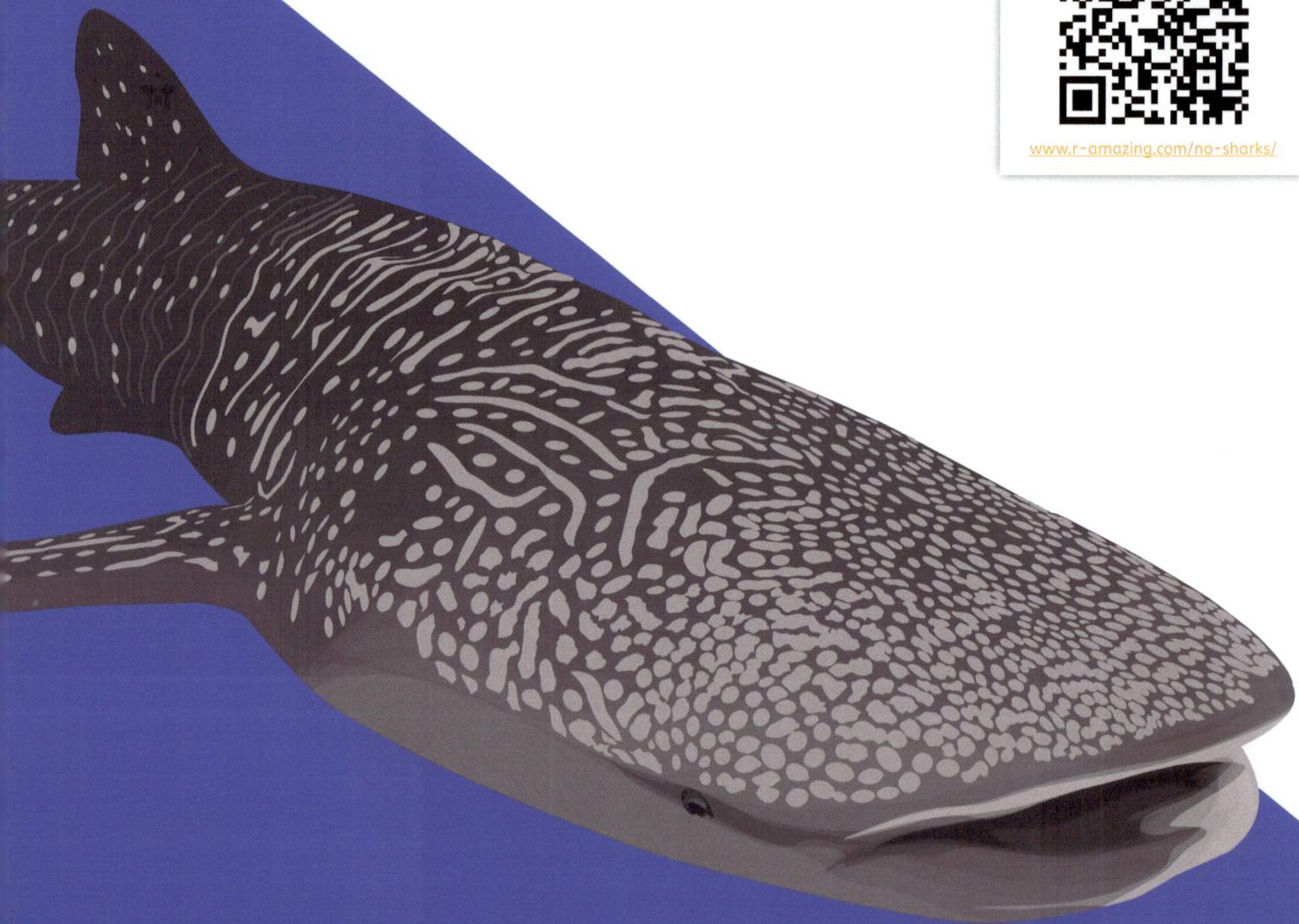

No Sharks?

Shockingly around 25% of all shark species are at risk of extinction, which means they could disappear forever.

There are now 90% less sharks in the world than there were 50 years ago, for example, if there were 1,000,000 sharks half a century ago, today there would be only 100,000.

Humans are shark's only real predators, we kill them out of fear, for profit or to eat. Our overfishing also causes the death of many sharks because it reduces the amount of food available for them to survive.

Sharks have been at the top of their food chain for hundreds of millions of years and should they disappear the effect it has on the world's eco-system could be horrendous.

The survival of sharks is in our hands and we can make changes that will ensure they, and our planet, will still be here for future generations to see and experience.

DID YOU KNOW?

Sharks are found in every ocean on the planet.
The Bull sharks can also live in both fresh and saltwater.

Source: https://www.sharksider.com/50-amazing-shark-facts/

A Shark in a fish tank will grow to 8 inches, But in the ocean, it will grow to 8 ft or more. The Shark will never outgrow its environment.

Bob Harrison

Lifesaver

Whilst on holiday in California, 39-year-old Eugene Finney went for a swim in the sea, when all of sudden he felt a large impact on his back. Feeling in pain and shock he left the sea. It was only then that he realised he had been bitten by a shark.

Eugene's shark bite was treated locally and he went home to Fitchburg, Massachusetts for it to heal.

He continued to struggle with pain caused by the attack so he visited his local doctor who discovered a stage one walnut-sized tumour on his right kidney.

Eugene had the growth removed and is now cancer free.

The shark attack led to a situation that saved his life. That's pretty fascinating when you think about it.

Dr. Ingolf Tuerk

Giving Birth

There are many odd traits when it comes to sharks giving birth.

Whilst still in the womb, some baby sharks even fight and eat their siblings. Researchers believe this happens when the mother is carrying babies from more than one father at the same time. The baby pups that are born tend to all be from the same father. It can be like gang warfare inside the mother, with the strongest offspring from one father surviving.

Mother sharks tend to lose their appetite before giving birth. This is to stop them from eating their pups. This loss of appetite overruns their built-in response to eat smaller prey. As soon as they are born the babies swim off and take care of themselves, before their mother's hunger returns.

Amazingly, in 2001, a female hammerhead shark at a Zoo in Nebraska shocked her keepers when she gave birth. This is because she had been in captivity and had never mixed with a male shark to create the babies. Researchers call this parthenogenesis, which means that the shark cloned herself to create her babies.

Without sharks, you take away the apex predator of the ocean, and you destroy the entire food chain.

Peter Benchley

DID YOU KNOW?

Even though sharks are known as fish they differ from all other fishes in the following ways:

- Sharks have cartilage instead of a skeleton.
- Sharks have eyelids.
- Unlike fish, sharks can only swim forward.
- Sharks have a larger brain than fish.
- Sharks have smooth placoid scales to help them swim much faster than fish.

Source: https://www.sharksider.com/50-amazing-shark-facts/

Dolphins and Sharks

Some surfers and open water swimmers have believed that if you see dolphins, there will be no sharks in the same area. Shark expert, Andrew Nosal, debunked this when he shared that both sharks and dolphins hunt the same food meaning they are likely to be in the same places.

Eating the same food means that, at times, dolphins and sharks can compete and fight for food.

Dolphins have also been known to protect humans from shark attacks. In 2004, dolphins circled a lifeguard who was swimming with his daughter to drive a shark away from the pair.

> *Don't trust blindly. If in shark infested waters, don't assume the fin coming toward you is a dolphin.*
>
> Mary Russel

Shark's Friend

In 2001, whilst on holiday with his wife, Krishna Thompson's leg was grabbed by a shark who pulled him underwater and away from the beach.

Realising that he had to do something to save his life he punched the shark on the nose twice and pulled open its mouth. This was enough for him to escape and get back to the shore.

The attack resulted in the amputation of Krishna's leg. You may imagine that Krishna has a dislike of sharks for what one did to him, but you would be incorrect. For he is now a shark advocate who raises the profile of how their preservation is so important to keep the whole ocean in balance.

> *Yes, you lost a leg but you have a whole other leg. You have two arms. You can walk.*
>
> Krishna Thompson

DID YOU KNOW?

A group of sharks is called a gam, herd, frenzy, school or shiver.

Source: https://www.sharks-world.com/what_is_a_group_of_sharks_called/

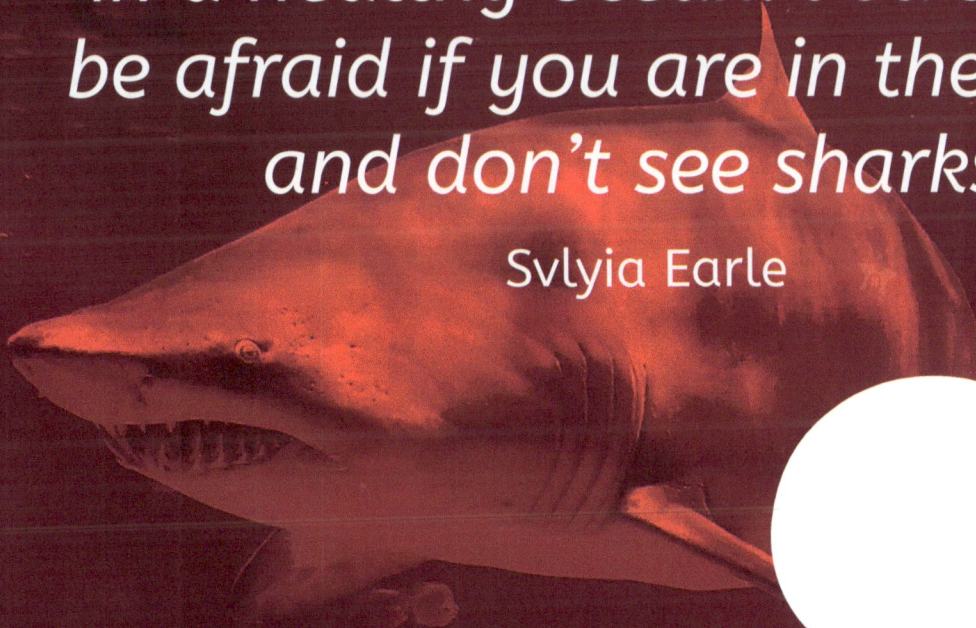

Sharks are beautiful animals, and if you are lucky enough to see them, that means you are in a healthy ocean. You should be afraid if you are in the ocean and don't see sharks.

Svlyia Earle

Swim Like A Shark

In 2004, NASA scientists and researchers looked to develop a swimsuit to help us swim faster. They chose to replicate the skin of a shark to reduce the friction and drag of the swimmer.

This resulted in the creation of the Speedo LZR swimsuit which covered most of the body like a wet suit. Within months of its release in early 2008, athletes who wore the LZR swimsuit broke an amazing 13 world records.

At the 2008 Beijing Olympics, 98% of the swimmers who won medals and 23 out of the 25 swimmers who broke world records were wearing a LZR swimsuit. In 2009, this resulted with the world governing body of swimming (FINA) banning the use of the LZR suit from all competitions.

The LZR swimsuit helps us realise just how efficiently sharks have evolved to swim and glide through the water.

"
Shark are born swimming.
Ben Stiller
"

"

Sharks never stop swimming;
that's when they die.
You gotta keep moving.

Reggie Miller

DID YOU KNOW?

Sharks have survived four of the "big five" mass extinctions. This makes them older than humanity, older than Mount Everest, older than dinosaurs, and even older than trees.

My picture of the most amazing shark in the world!

The most amazing shark in the world is

. . . .

I love it when this amazing shark...

....

....

....

....

....

....

This shark is amazing because...

....

....

....

....

MORE BOOKS BY R&Q

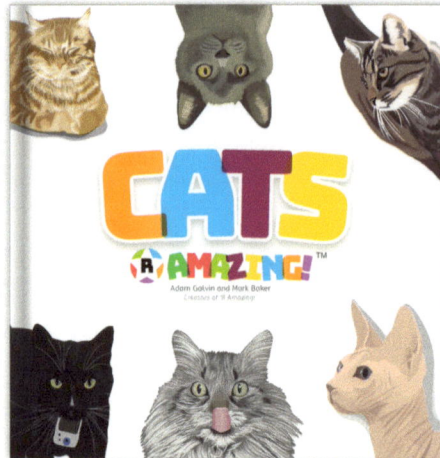

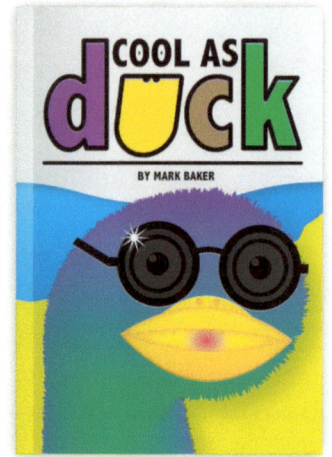

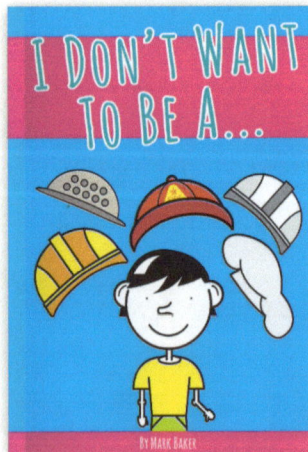

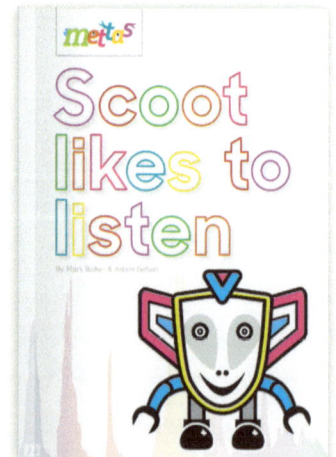

DOOR KNOB FOR A NOSE
BY MARK BAKER & JENNIFER BAKER

CATS R AMAZING!
Adam Galvin and Mark Baker
Creators of 'R Amazing'

COOL AS duck
BY MARK BAKER

I DON'T WANT TO BE A...
BY MARK BAKER

THIS BOOK NEVER ENDS...
...it keeps looping round and round until somebody says "PLEASE STOP READING NOW!"
Who is going to give up first? The grown up or the child because...
By Mark Baker

meltos
Scoot likes to listen
By Mark Baker & Adam Galvin

check out the books and merchandise at

w w w . R - a n d - Q . c o m